The Croft Tearoom

2007 – 2015

Carole Wells

Published in 2016 by Cray 150 Publications

Copyright © Carole Wells

The right of the author to be identified as author of this work has been asserted in accordance with the Copyright, Designs & Patents Act 1988.

ISBN 9780956829382

All rights reserved. No part of this publication may be reproduced, stored in a retrieval system, or transmitted in any form or by any means, electronic, mechanical, photocopying, recording or otherwise, without the prior permission in writing of the publishers.

Printed by Catford Print Centre

"There are few hours in life more agreeable than the hour dedicated to the ceremony known as afternoon tea."
Henry James: *The Portrait of a Lady*.

"There is no trouble so great or grave that cannot be much diminished by a nice cup of tea."
Bernard-Paul Heroux.

I dedicate this book to my mum, Marjorie Chisholm, who was the inspiration behind the Tearoom. She worked in customer services all her life and taught me the joy of serving other people.

Acknowledgements & Thanks

My sincere thanks and gratitude go to:-

1 My staff who supported me over the years and worked so hard to make the Croft what it has become. Special thanks go to Jenny and April who both made a huge contribution.

2 All our volunteers who gave their time and skills (nearly 100 of them over the years!) Special thanks go to Christine, Fatou, Barbara, Helen, Steve, Liz and Judy.

3 Our Trustees who supported me through difficult times, notably David, Paul, Maggy and Jo.

4 Our Sponsors, who donated so generously to help us pay for new equipment and essential repairs.

5 Our community leaders, organisations and local Councillors who continually supported us. Special thanks go to Jim and Jacky Cook.

6 All our lovely customers, - without whose custom, loyalty and friendship we would not have continued! Special thanks to all our regulars - too many to list but you know who you are! Jean, Ted, Sarah, Anne, David and Peter to mention just a few.

7 My family, especially Norman who helped me make some difficult decisions and dealt with all the building works, equipment and finances (with my sister-in-law Sue and my step-daughter Stephanie). To my sister, Diane, who supported me as

only sisters can. And to Katie who had to cope with a mum who was absent or preoccupied most of the time. I love you all.

8 All my friends who travelled with me on this journey and supported me through the many ups and downs. Special thanks go to Maggy, Viv, Marie-Therese, the St John's Mums and the Bromley Working Mothers' Group.

9 Rebecca for taking on the demanding role of owner/manager and the challenge of running the business from 2015.

10 Final thanks go to Jerry Dowlen who suggested writing this little book and for his help in compiling and producing it.

It was an absolute pleasure working with you all and I look forward to enjoying some lovely tea and cake at the Tearoom - as a customer from now on!

Carole Wells
Founder, Owner & Manager 2007 – 2015

"I want to open a Tearoom."

That bold announcement in 2007 led Carole Wells to open her beloved Croft Tearoom in November 2009. In rapid time it became a much-loved and award-winning local community institution in St Mary Cray High Street.

Five years later, with nearly 5,000 customers coming through the door annually, the Tearoom was assuredly delivering its owner's objectives - to provide quality food and service and to add value to the community.

But then came a dilemma for Carole. She and her husband Norman wanted to retire in mid-2015. The Tearoom had a popular past – but did it have a promising future?

Please read on and enjoy in words and pictures Carole's story of the Croft Tearoom from 2007 to 2015.

Contents

13   Forewords

19   The Croft Tearoom – My Story

39   Aunties, Cakes and Menus!

53   Producers' Spotlight

61   Popular Events, Talks and Performers

66   Artwork and Books

70   Poems

75   Retirement and Relaunch

81   Press Coverage of the Croft Tearoom

93   Tearoom Timeline

99   Last Pour from the Teapot …

Foreword (1)
Jim Cook

Jim Cook is Chairman and Planning Officer of the St Mary Cray Action Group.

I first met Carole Wells seven years ago when she came to one of our Action Group meetings and gave a short presentation to us, explaining that she was proposing to open a new Tearoom. It was to be a 'social enterprise' and was to be built on the site of an existing, rather decrepit, small building on the corner of Red Lion Close in St Mary Cray High Street. From recollection her proposal received almost universal support from our members.

Carole's proposal was eventually accepted by Bromley Council but without the training area that she had originally envisaged. From my first meeting with Carole and from observing the enterprise that she was keen to initiate, it was clear to me that Carole was a community-minded person. Her community credentials were further enhanced when the public house next door to the Tearoom and the pharmacy opposite both became empty. Carole was hoping that these two premises could be brought into community ownership. This unfortunately did not come to fruition, but the effort was instrumental in energising community activity, because its consequence was the formation of the Cray Village Community Forum which is still a functioning entity today.

Carole was also keen to set up a Country Market in St Mary Cray to work in conjunction with the Tearoom. Both in due course were opened at around the same time in 2009. Carole's husband Norman was an active member and treasurer.

Carole should be justly proud of all that she has achieved and sought to achieve for us in St Mary Cray since she opened the Tearoom. Now in new hands, the Croft Tearoom remains a key focal point and asset and we should all be thankful to Carole for the superb contribution that she has made to our local area and our community.

Foreword (2)
Colin Maclean

Colin Maclean is Chief Executive of Community Links Bromley 'Supporting Voluntary Action'.

Carole and I share three very similar passions – social enterprise, volunteering and cakes! The last one is mainly because we both suffer from the same condition – a Scottish sweet tooth!

In case you don't know about Community Links Bromley - we are the lead agency in Bromley for the voluntary, community and social enterprise sector. We run the Volunteer Centre in South Street.

When I first started over three years ago, I was interested to find out about social enterprises operating across Bromley. I soon came across Carole and the Croft. Like many others I was impressed with what had already been achieved but also that they had won the Bromley Business Award for Commitment to the Community in 2011 … after only two years of operation!

On volunteering, Community Links Bromley has worked with the Croft since 2009 when we started to engage with Carole to develop their programme. They have registered numerous types of volunteering roles and recruited around 100 volunteers over the last five years. The majority came via CLB. We have always felt confident in referring potential volunteers to the Tearoom. We know that they will be well received and that the processes for recruitment are robust and equitable.

Many volunteers have benefitted from adding this experience to their CV. I know that this has led to at least three people being employed at the Croft. For such a modest venture to make such an impact on the lives of local people is massively important. So I am a great fan of the Croft Tearoom. It is a shining light for the voluntary, community and social enterprise sector. I can't think of a better example of a champion for local volunteering. I am full of thanks to Carole and her team for what they have achieved.

Foreword (3)
Jerry Dowlen

Jerry Dowlen is a local author and community leader.

I speak for two local organisations that have come to rely on the Croft Tearoom. These are Cray Wanderers Football Club and the Croft Poetry Club. It surely speaks volumes about the Tearoom's admirable extent of engagement with our community that one of those organisations is 155 years old, while the other is just over one year old.

And those two organisations that I happen to be associated with are just a tip of the iceberg: there are numerous other local interest groups and associations both commercial and social that have caught on to Carole's community vision and have adopted the Tearoom as a most enjoyable and effective hub from which to operate.

I especially commend the Tearoom for its role as an arts and heritage hub. It is my belief that within our locality we harbour a number of very talented artists, musicians and writers. We've got people who sing; people who play and write music; people who love to write stories, poems and memoirs; people who love to paint or do craftwork, ceramics, glasswork and pottery; people who are keen photographers. It's great that the Tearoom showcases their work.

This new book *The Croft Tearoom* is surely a 'must': a book by Carole and for Carole so that the originating history of St Mary Cray's most popular Tearoom can be celebrated by us all in words and pictures.

The Croft Tearoom – My Story

"A Tearoom will never work in St Mary Cray - it makes no commercial sense!" – words of wisdom from my husband Norman as I pondered over the 'For Sale' sign in the High Street.

Having run our own businesses in Bromley for 25 years, my 'business' head agreed with him; but my heart felt differently and my thoughts kept returning to this little shop at no. 263, in need of some TLC and investment.

I had been looking for a new direction for some time and felt I wanted to do something that would make a difference in a community which needed it. So, could a Tearoom work in St Mary Cray? After much thought we decided that it could: but only if it operated very differently from the average café!

Enter the world of the 'CIC' a Community Interest Company: set up for the benefit of the community it serves and run as a commercial (not-for-profit) business with social aims. Our existing business, Circa Ltd, purchased the premises in 2008 and financed its rebuild.

A specialist conservation architect designed the new wooden building in the style of the 19th century shop that had stood on that site for over 100 years. *(For more information, see the History Timeline at page 93).*

Gaining planning consent from Bromley Council for the design and change of use was a lengthy process as the building was in one of the St Mary Cray conservation areas, but although smaller than we wanted, consent was finally granted.

As a community enterprise, we started by working with a local building project for young people based in St Paul's Cray, who helped us demolish the old building (which had no foundations!) and recycle as much of the original materials as possible. Using a number of local builders, it was finally completed with Victorian roof tiles on the top!

The interior decor was based on the colours in a William Morris pattern called 'Cray' which can be seen on the window-blind pictured on page 19. I discovered through my research that the renowned Victorian artist designed a range of patterns named after local rivers when he lived in 'The Red House' in Bexley (now owned by the National Trust). The aubergine and green colours in 'Cray' were even used for our aprons and cruet sets!

Next, we had to decide on a name........ We played around with words connected to the area and as we discussed this in bed one Saturday morning we had a 'light bulb' moment. Why not call it 'The Croft' which linked the 'Rosecroft' area of the High Street to my Scottish heritage, where a croft was a small farm holding where people gathered together to live, work and eat.

Photos, below and next page:
The building old, under construction, and new.

The vision and ethos of the Croft Tearoom CIC was very clear to Norman and me. It had to be run on three founding principles: 1) To serve high quality, home-made food; 2) To give great customer service; and 3) To serve our community, adding something of value to the High Street.

I visited many local community groups to talk about my ideas for the Tearoom as well as the launch of the new St Mary Cray Country Market that I was also setting up, because it tied in with our passion for local produce.

Jim Cook, John Breach and a young Volunteer.

Following these consultations, long-lasting partnerships and ongoing friendships were forged with the amazing community leaders and residents that I met – dedicated people all committed to improving their community and preserving its history and heritage. These included: The SMC Action Group, Cray Valley Friends of the Parks, Safer Neighbourhood team, Bromley Gypsy Traveller Project, Churches, Schools, Bromley Council (parks, renewal & health), local Councillors, WI's and many more. Later in 2011 we went on to form the CVCF (Cray Village Community Forum), a representative group of local organisations and residents' associations to plan a vision and development project for the Crays.

I had no experience of running catering businesses (other than waitressing as a student!) but I knew I wanted volunteers to be part of the team so I volunteered myself for 6 months at the Age Concern café in West Wickham to gain experience. This opened my eyes to the value of volunteering, both for the organisation and the individual; and I formed an ongoing partnership with CLB (Community Links Bromley) who supplied most of our volunteers thereafter.

A year was spent sourcing small local food producers and farms in Kent and the southern home counties. This was a fascinating and highly enjoyable process as Norman and I visited each site, met the producers and farmers, discussed the sourcing of their ingredients and observed the production of their amazing, delicious produce. We visited cheese makers, fruit farms, bread makers (including Paul Hollywood's business before he got really famous!), beekeepers, butchers, meat & fish smokeries, rapeseed oil & crisp makers, fudge makers, jam and chutney makers, dairy farms and greengrocers.

teas • home made cakes • pastries • soups • locally sourced produce
www.crofttearoom.co.uk   tea@crofttearoom.co.uk

Carole at the Harris Hospice Care Fair.

Maggy Flook and Viv Barker at the Cray Festival.

I knew very little about leaf teas so during this time I went on a course run by the Tea Council in London which was incredibly informative and taught me all about the different teas and their history. We visited a 'Tea Master' in Bromley and tasted more than twenty teas before selecting the shortlist for our menu. We sourced the teas from his recommended tea merchant in Hampshire. Being a bit of a coffee connoisseur Norman helped me choose one of the best coffee suppliers we could find in London - the Monmouth Coffee company who roast their own ethically-sourced beans.

The Croft Tearoom CIC was getting ready to launch and the next step was to gather a good team together. I recruited two part-time Cooks and a team of Volunteers (including myself in the role of Manager/Front of House). The following year I recruited an Apprentice Kitchen Assistant and we went on in later years to offer two further Apprenticeships in professional catering and leadership.

Jenny and Carole with Helen and Claire in 2011.

Fatou and Jenny

Christine

The menu was agreed; the kitchen was equipped; the shop area was stocked up and we opened on 12th November 2009 with the Mayor of Bromley and the local newspaper in attendance!

Carole with the Mayor, Cllr. Douglas Auld.

Viv and Maggy cleaning the windows!

The winter of 2009 was harsh, with thick snow in December but the Tearoom stayed open and staff managed to walk into work, although at worst it took me four hours to get home by car!

The year 2009 was also when the worst recession for decades began: add the disruption caused by major road works in the High Street and altogether it was not the best time to have started our new business!

The Croft was tucked away off the main shopping areas with few other shops nearby so after a few months I realised that we would have to diversify our range of services if we were to survive. We had built up a loyal following of regular customers, mostly local people many of whom were older/retired, walkers, cyclists, women's groups, Church groups, special needs, younger couples and families. They told us that they liked coming to the Croft because of our friendly welcome, good food and because they could chat to other customers in a relaxed atmosphere. Single people told us that they felt very comfortable coming in on their own.

We were different to the chain cafés and I realised that it was this difference that made us special and unique.

Building on this knowledge we began to run our first events in the evenings and during the daytimes. Through talking with customers I discovered a wealth of talent in St Mary Cray - musicians, singers, dancers, historians, authors and special interest groups. So ... would they be willing to perform for us at one of our events for the benefit of local people in our community? I asked them and they said yes! We decided to offer three-course dinners with the evening entertainment and afternoon teas with the daytime events.

Thus, our 'performance arts and events programme' began and continued over the following years to be a major part of our ethos (and income!). Events have included: Musical Nights (Barber Shop, Jazz, Folk, Classical, Opera, Musical Theatre, Burns Suppers, Ukulele, Acoustic Guitar, Crooners and Irish bands), Dance events (Morris, Arabian Belly dancing!), regular Quiz Nights, Ladies Pamper Evenings - and who could forget the carol-singing at our Christmas lunches from the local primary school children and the seniors from Riverside School?

Daytime events also proved very popular with our Tea & Talk programme covering local authors' book talks, local history talks and special interest groups including the Orpington Archaeological Society, Ferns of St Mary Cray and the Cray Wanderers Football Club. Some now meet at the Tearoom on a regular basis, including the Croft Poetry Group and the Croft Book Club.

Arabian Nights

Jazz with the Dave Silk Trio

Joanna Friel from the Chislehurst Society.

Sue Campbell talking about Lilian Snelling MBE the world-renowned botanical artist who was born in St Mary Cray in 1879 and died there in 1972. Her work was exhibited in Edinburgh and at Kew Gardens in London. She was awarded the Victoria Medal in 1955.

During our first year we also diversified into outside catering. We were asked by local churches (most notably All Saints), charities, other local community groups, businesses and residents to provide a range of catering options for their events - and so we did!

This service grew over the following years and, along with our internal events, it continued to sustain the Tearoom. We launched a second CIC - Croft Events Catering CIC in 2013.

Cheese, fruit and biscuits

My passion for community service and local produce won us three small grants as well as some awards. The first grant came from the Lottery funded 'Awards4All' and helped us pave the courtyard area and entrance ramp to make them more wheelchair-friendly. This also paid for the signage on the front of the building and new marketing leaflets. The second grant from Affinity Sutton enabled us to recruit an Activities Organiser, Sarah Jeffries, to set up and run a range of community events, including 'Zumba@theChurch', a community choir, a power-walking group and the 'Tea & Toast' parents support group.

Zumba Club at the Big O festival in Orpington. Sarah Jeffries 2nd from right.

Community Choir at the Big O Festival.

The third grant from Sustain helped us to launch our 'Passion for Bread' service – nurturing Maria, a local resident, to set up her own micro-business making handmade, artisan bread – a first in Bromley! *(See the Producers' Spotlight on page 59)*.

Our Community Awards included:

2013: Runners-up Bromley Business 'Entrepreneur of the Year'
2012: Finalists South London Business
2011: Winner Bromley Business 'Commitment to the Community'
2011: Overall Winner of all ten Bromley awards that year
2010: Winner Bromley Environmental for 'Sustainability'

Suzanne Sharp, group sales manager at News Shopper, with Carole Wells, director of The Croft Tearoom CIC

Maggy Flook (Trustee), Tom Hart-Dyke, Norman Wells

The Croft Tea Room in St Mary Cray won the Business Award and was also named the overall winner on the night

Constant marketing and a growing customer database were critical to our growth and by 2015 we had nearly 5,000 customers coming through our doors each year. We were predominantly serving a local community: analysis of our customer database revealed that 60% - 70% were regulars from BR5 & BR6 postcodes.

We welcomed customers too from Bromley areas as far away as Beckenham and Penge; and further afield from Bexley, Greenwich, London and Kent.

After eight years of setting up and running the Croft, and the full-time commitment this involved, I felt it was time to step back and hand over the reins to a new owner / manager. My passion and enthusiasm for the business was still strong but my energy levels were waning and my long-suffering family had tolerated my total absorption in the project long enough!

Finding the right person willing to take over the whole business was difficult, not least because of the lack of any funds to pay a manager's salary! Also, the commitment, time, responsibility and skills needed were a tall order.

After exploring various options for the future of the Croft I finally decided early in 2015 that the time had come for me to 'retire' and that my only option was to close the business. So, with an extremely heavy heart I emailed all our customers, colleagues and friends with the news.

Contrary to my expectations, I received over 90 emails expressing dismay and shock at my decision. Several individuals and organisations contacted me to discuss taking over the business to ensure that the Tearoom remained open! At the 11th hour (like a gift) it appeared that the Croft would be saved and Rebecca Birs stepped up to the challenge.

As a local resident, business woman and customer, Rebecca cared about St Mary Cray and felt (like I did) that the Croft played a vital part in the community. After a transitional three months of our handing over the reins, Rebecca took on the ownership and management of the business in July 2015.

I am proud to think that the Croft Tearoom CIC now plays its small part in the history and heritage of St Mary Cray. I hope you enjoy reading about the project and that you continue to enjoy great food, service, events and companionship at the Croft!

Rebecca and Carole, May 2015.

Aunties, Cakes and Menus!

As a child, I had sampled the delights of my Scottish aunties' home-baking (with melt-in-the-mouth shortbread, meringues and cakes 'to die for') and since then I have been a sucker for home-made cakes, always seeking out the WI or Church tea stalls where I knew good home-bakers thrived. I borrowed Auntie Mag's handwritten recipe book and gathered other cake recipes from members of my extended family.

For the menu, I based a lot of choices on what my mum would like if she were a customer - very soft bread, thick egg mayo, lots of cress, warm scones and homemade soups!

After searching far and wide we found Roland's Bakery in Green St Green who baked lovely white and brown sandwich breads, far superior to any supermarket. Free range eggs and high quality mayonnaise were sourced locally plus further recipes for soups, which had to be seasonal. Norman came from a jam-making family so he became chief jam-maker and supplier to the Tearoom providing us with seasonal selections including blackberry jelly and wild greengage jam as well as delicious raspberry. He also made our popular elderflower cordial served with sparkling water.

Gradually, the menu was compiled to include as much locally produced ingredients as we could find from the lovely suppliers we had visited. The first menu has been overtaken through time but on the next three pages we reprint a copy of our menu from around 2010/11 and much of the original items live on!

Drinks

Croft Tea Blend (regular builders tea)
Mug - £1.00   Pot for 1 - £1.50   Pot for 2 - £2.70

Leaf Teas	Pot for 1	Pot for 2
Assam (Behora GFBOP)	£1.85	£3.50
Indian – strong black tea		
Darjeeling (Badamtan mid)	£1.85	£3.50
Indian – medium black tea		
Ceylon (Uva full leaf)	£1.80	£3.40
Sri-Lankan – delicate black tea		
Earl Grey	£1.80	£3.40
Classic -scented with bergamot		
Green Tea (Gunpowder)	£1.75	£3.30
China– delicate, young green tea		
Jasmine Green Tea	£1.75	£3.30
China – mixed with jasmine blossoms		
White Tea (Pai Mu Tan)	£1.95	£3.75
China – delicate - the 'white wine' of teas!		
Oolong (Ti Kuan Yin)	£1.95	£3.75
China's favourite aromatic mid green & black tea		
Lapsang Souchong (Osprey)	£1.95	£3.75
China black distinctly smokey		
Guest Tea		See Board

Flower/Fruit/Herbal & Infusions	Pot for 1
Rooibos (SF Leaf)	£1.75
South African – caffeine free 'Bush Tea' as drunk by the No.1 Ladies Detective!	
Peppermint Leaf	£1.70
China Green Tea	
Chamomile (bag)	£1.50
Fruit Tea (bag)	£1.50

Served with Milk, Soya Milk, Lemon or Honey

Our Teas are chosen for their quality of taste, appearance & pure ingredients and are supplied by, 'All About Tea' Merchants, from teas picked from ethical plantations

Coffee   Per Cup
Our Coffee is produced from very high quality, award winning beans sourced from ethical coffee plantations, roasted by The Monmouth Coffee Company in London and selected for their strength & flavour

Americano	£1.90
(black coffee – espresso + extra hot water served with milk)	
Café Latte	£2.10
(very milky - espresso mixed with steamed & frothed milk)	
Cappuccino	£2.10
(espresso topped with frothy milk & organic cocoa powder)	
Mocha Coffee	£2.75
(Hot chocolate with a double espresso)	
Espresso	£1.70
(double shot of the strong stuff with 'crema' on top)	
Iced Coffee	£2.20
(Double espresso & chilled milk on the rocks!)	

Hot Chocolate   Mug - £2.20
(made with Green & Blacks Organic Hot Chocolate and milk)

Topped with **Whipped Cream**	extra 30p
Topped with **Marshmallows**	extra 25p

Cold Drinks

Home-made Fruit Cordials & Sparkling Water	£1.70
(Elderflower or Lime & Ginger)	
Kentish Apple Juice	per glass - £1.85
Kentish Pear Juice (organic)	per glass - £1.95
Kentish Mixed Fruit Juice Bottles	£1.75
Orange Juice	per glass - £1.80
Fentimans Victorian Lemonade	£1.80
Fentimans Ginger Beer	£1.80
Fentimans Dandelion & Burdock	£1.80
Mineral Water *(Sparkling)*	per glass - £1.00

Food

Hot Food

Croft Cooked Breakfast £4.75
Kent free range 90% meat sausage, 2 bacon rashers, scrambled egg, baked beans, roast cherry tomatoes, 1 slice toast & butter

Porridge £1.80
Organic English oats served with milk & brown sugar

Home-made Rosehip Syrup or Honey   Extra 60p

Toast
2 slices of locally made granary or white   £1.80
(Served warm with butter)
Home-made Jam or Marmalade   Extra 60p
Local Honey, Peanut Butter or Marmite   Extra 60p
Baked Beans on 2 slices of toast   £2.95
Eggs on 2 slices of toast   £2.95
(scrambled, poached or boiled)
Kentish Cheese *(1 or 2 slices)*   £2.75 / £4.95
(toasted + cherry tomato garnish)
Croft on Horseback *(1 or 2 slices)*   £3.25 / £5.95
toasted Kent cheese + poached egg on top!
Extra Sausage   £1.30
Extra Bacon Rasher   £1.00
Mix in some Smoked Salmon   Extra £2.00
for a little luxury!

Omelettes
(2 eggs served with bread & butter and salad garnish)
Plain   £3.95
With 1 Filling (see list)   £4.95
Extra Filling   £1.00

Jacket Potatoes *(with butter & salad garnish)*
Plain   £2.95
With 1 Filling (see list)   £3.95
Extra Filling   £1.00

Home-made Soup of the Day   £3.75
(Seasonal vegetable with granary bread & butter)

Hot Lunch of the Day   **ASK or SEE BOARD**

Cold Food

Sandwiches
(All our sandwiches are made to order with locally-made Bread – granary or white, using butter not margarine)

Egg Mayo & Cress (Kent free range)   £2.95
Hummous, Grated Carrot & Cucumber   £3.10
Tuna Mayo & Cucumber   £3.25
Kent Cheese   £3.75
(full flavour Kentish cheese with tomato, cucumber or hand-made pickle)
Kent Meaty Sausage   £3.75
(with tomato ketchup, brown sauce or mayo)
Smoked Bacon   £3.75
(with tomato ketchup, brown sauce or mayo)
Sussex Ham   £3.75
(with Sussex mustard or tomatoes)
Smoked Chicken   £3.95
(with home-made coleslaw, pickles or salad)
Smoked Salmon & Cream Cheese   £4.25
(Scottish salmon smoked at the Weald Smokery in Kent)

Toasted Sandwiches
All our sandwiches are available toasted - for an Extra 25p!

Warm Wraps *(new!)*   £3.50
(with Roast Vegetables and cream cheese or hummous)

Kent Crisps   75p
(Sea Salt, Biddenden Cider Vinegar, Kent Cheese & Onion)

Platters   £5.95
(Served with bread & butter, home-made coleslaw & pickles and salad garnish)
Smoked Chicken / Sussex Ham / Tuna & Egg / Kent Cheese

Croft Ploughmans   £7.50
(A selection of English fare including cheeses, hand-made pickles & seasonal fruit served with traditional oatcakes)

Please note that our products may contain nuts.
Please let us know if you have any allergies or concerns and we will be happy to advise you

Sweet

Cream Tea — £4.50

Pot of Tea or Cup of Coffee *(Americano)*
2 warm home-made Scones with butter, home made jam & cream

Afternoon Tea — £8.95
(Served on a cake stand)

Pot of Tea or Cup of Coffee *(Americano)*
Finger Sandwiches
(cucumber & cream cheese, egg & cress, tuna mayo or ham salad)
Scone with **butter, home-made jam & cream**
Cake of your choice

Croft Special Kentish Tea — £10.95
(Served on a cake stand)

Glass of Sparkling home-made Cordial
Pot of Tea or Cup of Coffee of your choice
Smoked Salmon & Cream Cheese Sandwiches
(or smoked chicken & home-made coleslaw)
2 Scones with **butter, home-made jam & cream**
Cake of your choice

Ice Cream — £2.50
(Hand made in Kent from 100% natural ingredients by Simply Ice Cream. See list of our favourite flavours!)

Cakes
(A selection of delicious Cakes made by our Cook & team of Home-Bakers)

Cake of The Day — See Board
(Our changing daily special)

Scones — £2.50
(2 plain or fruit - baked in our kitchen, served warm with butter & home-made jam)

Tea Bread — £2.25
(the old favourite and still the best - served with butter)

Shortbread (2) — £1.60
(Award winning Scottish recipe)

All our Cakes are available whole (to order)
Kent Ice Cream from our shop £1.80 per tub

Please note that our products may contain nuts.
Please let us know if you have any allergies or concerns and we will be happy to advise you.

Menu favourites and buffets served up by the Croft Tearoom cooks

Apple filo tart

Drinks

Croft Tea Blend (regular builders tea)
Mug - £1.00   Pot for 1 - £1.50   Pot for 2 - £2.70

Leaf Teas	Pot for 1	Pot for 2
Assam (Behora GFBOP)	£1.85	£3.50
Indian – strong black tea		
Darjeeling (Badamtan mid)	£1.85	£3.50
Indian – medium black tea		
Ceylon (Uva full leaf)	£1.80	£3.40
Sri-Lankan – delicate black tea		
Earl Grey	£1.80	£3.40
Classic -scented with bergamot		
Green Tea (Gunpowder)	£1.75	£3.30
China– delicate, young green tea		
Jasmine Green Tea	£1.75	£3.30
China – mixed with jasmine blossoms		
White Tea (Pai Mu Tan)	£1.95	£3.75
China – delicate - the 'white wine' of teas!		
Oolong (Ti Kuan Yin)	£1.95	£3.75
China's favourite aromatic mid green & black tea		
Lapsang Souchong (Osprey)	£1.95	£3.75
China black distinctly smokey		
Guest Tea		See Board

Flower/Fruit/Herbal & Infusions	Pot for 1
Rooibos (SF Leaf)	£1.75
South African – caffeine free 'Bush Tea' as drunk by the No.1 Ladies Detective!	
Peppermint Leaf	£1.70
China Green Tea	
Chamomile (bag)	£1.50
Fruit Tea (bag)	£1.50

Served with Milk, Soya Milk, Lemon or Honey

Our Teas are chosen for their quality of taste, appearance & pure ingredients and are supplied by, 'All About Tea' Merchants, from teas picked from ethical plantations

Coffee   Per Cup
Our Coffee is produced from very high quality, award winning beans sourced from ethical coffee plantations, roasted by The Monmouth Coffee Company in London and selected for their strength & flavour

Americano	£1.90
(black coffee – espresso + extra hot water served with milk)	
Café Latte	£2.10
(very milky - espresso mixed with steamed & frothed milk)	
Cappuccino	£2.10
(espresso topped with frothy milk & organic cocoa powder)	
Mocha Coffee	£2.75
(Hot chocolate with a double espresso)	
Espresso	£1.70
(double shot of the strong stuff with 'crema' on top)	
Iced Coffee	£2.20
(Double espresso & chilled milk on the rocks!)	

Hot Chocolate   Mug - £2.20
(made with Green & Blacks Organic Hot Chocolate and milk)

Topped with **Whipped Cream**	extra 30p
Topped with **Marshmallows**	extra 25p

Cold Drinks

Home-made Fruit Cordials		£1.70
& Sparkling Water		
(Elderflower or Lime & Ginger)		
Kentish Apple Juice	per glass -	£1.85
Kentish Pear Juice (organic)	per glass -	£1.95
Kentish Mixed Fruit Juice Bottles		£1.75
Orange Juice	per glass -	£1.80
Fentimans Victorian Lemonade		£1.80
Fentimans Ginger Beer		£1.80
Fentimans Dandelion & Burdock		£1.80
Mineral Water	per glass -	£1.00
(Sparkling)		

Food

Hot Food

Croft Cooked Breakfast — £4.75
Kent free range 90% meat sausage, 2 bacon rashers, scrambled egg, baked beans, roast cherry tomatoes, 1 slice toast & butter

Porridge — £1.80
Organic English oats served with milk & brown sugar

Home-made Rosehip Syrup or Honey — Extra 60p

Toast
2 slices of locally made granary or white — £1.80
(Served warm with butter)
Home-made Jam or Marmalade — Extra 60p
Local Honey, Peanut Butter or Marmite — Extra 60p
Baked Beans on 2 slices of toast — £2.95
Eggs on 2 slices of toast — £2.95
(scrambled, poached or boiled)
Kentish Cheese (1 or 2 slices) — £2.75 / £4.95
(toasted + cherry tomato garnish)
Croft on Horseback (1 or 2 slices) — £3.25 / £5.95
toasted Kent cheese + poached egg on top!
Extra Sausage — £1.30
Extra Bacon Rasher — £1.00
Mix in some Smoked Salmon — Extra £2.00
for a little luxury!

Omelettes
(2 eggs served with bread & butter and salad garnish)
Plain — £3.95
With 1 Filling (see list) — £4.95
Extra Filling — £1.00

Jacket Potatoes *(with butter & salad garnish)*
Plain — £2.95
With 1 Filling (see list) — £3.95
Extra Filling — £1.00

Home-made Soup of the Day — £3.75
(Seasonal vegetable with granary bread & butter)

Hot Lunch of the Day   ASK or SEE BOARD

Cold Food

Sandwiches
(All our sandwiches are made to order with locally-made Bread – granary or white, using butter not margarine)

Egg Mayo & Cress (Kent free range) — £2.95
Hummous, Grated Carrot & Cucumber — £3.10
Tuna Mayo & Cucumber — £3.25
Kent Cheese — £3.75
(full flavour Kentish cheese with tomato, cucumber or hand-made pickle)
Kent Meaty Sausage — £3.75
(with tomato ketchup, brown sauce or mayo)
Smoked Bacon — £3.75
(with tomato ketchup, brown sauce or mayo)
Sussex Ham — £3.75
(with Sussex mustard or tomatoes)
Smoked Chicken — £3.95
(with home-made coleslaw, pickles or salad)
Smoked Salmon & Cream Cheese — £4.25
(Scottish salmon smoked at the Weald Smokery in Kent)

Toasted Sandwiches
All our sandwiches are available toasted - for an Extra 25p!

Warm Wraps *(new!)* — £3.50
(with Roast Vegetables and cream cheese or hummous)

Kent Crisps — 75p
(Sea Salt, Biddenden Cider Vinegar, Kent Cheese & Onion)

Platters — £5.95
(Served with bread & butter, home-made coleslaw & pickles and salad garnish)
Smoked Chicken / Sussex Ham / Tuna & Egg / Kent Cheese

Croft Ploughmans — £7.90
(A selection of English fare including cheeses, hand-made pickles & seasonal fruit served with traditional oatcakes)

Please note that our products may contain nuts.
Please let us know if you have any allergies or concerns and we will be happy to advise you

Sweet

Cream Tea — £4.50

Pot of Tea or **Cup of Coffee** *(Americano)*
2 warm home-made Scones with **butter, home made jam & cream**

Afternoon Tea — £8.95
(Served on a cake stand)

Pot of Tea or **Cup of Coffee** *(Americano)*
Finger Sandwiches
(cucumber & cream cheese, egg & cress, tuna mayo or ham salad)
Scone with **butter, home-made jam & cream**
Cake of your choice

Croft Special Kentish Tea — £10.95
(Served on a cake stand)

Glass of Sparkling home-made Cordial
Pot of Tea or **Cup of Coffee** of your choice
Smoked Salmon & Cream Cheese Sandwiches
(or smoked chicken & home-made coleslaw)
2 Scones with **butter, home-made jam & cream**
Cake of your choice

Ice Cream — £2.50
(Hand made in Kent from 100% natural ingredients by Simply Ice Cream. See list of our favourite flavours!)

Cakes
(A selection of delicious Cakes made by our Cook & team of Home-Bakers)

Cake of The Day — See Board
(Our changing daily special)

Scones — £2.50
(2 plain or fruit - baked in our kitchen, served warm with butter & home-made jam)

Tea Bread — £2.25
(the old favourite and still the best - served with butter)

Shortbread (2) — £1.60
(Award winning Scottish recipe)

All our Cakes are available whole (to order)
Kent Ice Cream from our shop £1.80 per tub

Please note that our products may contain nuts.
Please let us know if you have any allergies or concerns and we will be happy to advise you.

Menu favourites and buffets served up by the Croft Tearoom cooks

Apple filo tart

Sweet

Cream Tea £4.50

Pot of Tea or Cup of Coffee *(Americano)*
2 warm home-made Scones with **butter, home made jam & cream**

Afternoon Tea £8.95
(Served on a cake stand)

Pot of Tea or Cup of Coffee *(Americano)*
Finger Sandwiches
(cucumber & cream cheese, egg & cress, tuna mayo or ham salad)
Scone with **butter, home-made jam & cream**
Cake of your choice

Croft Special Kentish Tea £10.95
(Served on a cake stand)

Glass of Sparkling home-made Cordial
Pot of Tea or **Cup of Coffee** of your choice
Smoked Salmon & Cream Cheese Sandwiches
(or smoked chicken & home-made coleslaw)
2 Scones with **butter, home-made jam & cream**
Cake of your choice

Ice Cream £2.50
(Hand made in Kent from 100% natural ingredients by Simply Ice Cream. See list of our favourite flavours!)

Cakes
(A selection of delicious Cakes made by our Cook & team of Home-Bakers)

Cake of The Day .... See Board
(Our changing daily special)

Scones £2.50
(2 plain or fruit - baked in our kitchen, served warm with butter & home-made jam)

Tea Bread £2.25
(the old favourite and still the best - served with butter)

Shortbread (2) £1.60
(Award winning Scottish recipe)

All our Cakes are available whole (to order)
Kent Ice Cream from our shop £1.80 per tub

Please note that our products may contain nuts.
Please let us know if you have any allergies or concerns and we will be happy to advise you.

Menu favourites and buffets served up by the Croft Tearoom cooks

Apple filo tart

Buffet

Nibbles

Jams

Scones

Soup

Quiche – watercress & mushroom

Pasta

Thyme-roasted Chicken, Sussex Ham, Roast Beef

Cake selection *Elderflower cordial*

Victoria sponge

Recipes - two Tearoom favourites for you to try!

Kent Apple Cake (Sue Hayward)

12 oz SR Flour
Pinch salt
1 teaspoon baking powder
8oz butter
4oz sugar
4oz sultanas
1¼ lb cooking apples (peeled & cored weight)
3 eggs

Grease and flour an 8" round deep cake tin. Sift flour, salt & baking powder into bowl & rub in the fat until mixture resembles fine breadcrumbs. Stir in sugar & sultanas. Peel, core & cut apples into small dice sized pieces and mix into the dry ingredients. Lightly beat eggs & stir into mixture with a metal spoon – do not beat and no other liquid is needed. Turn into prepared tin. Bake in centre of moderate oven (350) for about 1-1.25 hours. Dust with castor sugar while still hot. (Do not make double this mixture as it is too hard to mix).

Best served warm.

Detling Tea Bread (W.I. – Country Markets)

½ pt strong, warm Tea
3 or 4oz Brown Sugar (I prefer 3oz)
12ozs Raisins
3oz Glace Cherries
1 Egg
8ozs SR Flour

Soak the fruits & sugar in the Tea overnight. Mix in the beaten egg & the flour. Line a 2lb loaf tin with baking parchment & fill with the cake mix. Bake at 160 c / Gas 3 for approx 1¼ hours or until an inserted skewer comes out cleanly. Cool on a wire rack.

Best served with butter and will keep well over a week.

Producers Spotlight

(1) Winterdale Cheesemakers

In April 2009 Carole and Norman first visited Robin and Carla Betts at their beautiful dairy farm situated high up on the North Downs near Wrotham, after reading about them in 'Produced in Kent' - a website full of small artisan food producers. The Betts family have been farming since 1495 and the dairy farm was set up in 1950 by Robin's grandfather! They started cheese-making in 2006 when Carla was pregnant with their first child, and since then they have gone on to win several world cheese awards. They now supply Fortnum & Mason – as well as the Croft Tearoom, of course!

Using milk from their own Friesian cows, they hand-make a traditional, unpasteurised cellar matured cheddar-style cheese called 'Winterdale Shaw' – full of flavour and strength. Carole and Norman thought it was perfect for the Croft menu - and it was regularly commented on favourably by customers, including children who, to the surprise of their parents, liked the taste of 'real cheese' instead of the rubbery supermarket options. A favourite choice was 'Croft on Horseback': toasted cheese with a poached egg on top!

Carole and some of the staff visited the farm again in 2014 to see the farm, learn more about the cheese-making process and visit the 'cave' where the cheeses are wrapped in muslin and stored for six months to mature. All members of the Betts family are involved in the business and it's an amazing 'cow to plate' story!

(2) Caregrow Fine Preserves

Carole first met Steve Page at the Eltham Farmers Market in early 2009. Supported by his wife Anne who works in IT software in midweek, Steve had started up his full-time home business in October 2007 after taking early retirement from international banking. At that time making jams, chutneys and cordials, soon to be followed by sauces, Steve now produces 30 varieties of jams. He sells his home produce at three south London markets and is a specialist supplier to a range of small local shops. Amongst his delicious home-made products there is his 'very special mulling syrup' – his unique recipe syrup for the Hatherwood brand of Winter Warmer Beer now stocked at Lidl.

Steve puts enormous emphasis on eco-friendly production of his locally-sourced foods. These, and Steve's warm, friendly character were a big factor in Carole inviting him to supply her Tearoom. Steve has installed solar power and he composts his waste ingredients. Crab apples, damsons and plums come from his own trees. Although he is based in built-up New Eltham he is a keen and knowledgeable woodlander: he knows where to find nearby blackberries, rosehips, sloes and wild greengages. "There is so much around!" – foraging for local ingredients grown in the wild is a labour of love for Steve.

Steve has won seven coveted 'Great Taste' awards: for three of his marmalades, three jams and his Quince Zing jelly. Steve and Carole are united in their experience and belief that "passion, enthusiasm and commitment are the essential pre-requisites for starting and running one's own business … and a lot of hard work of course!"

(3) Cray Village Honey

Grace and David Walton contacted Carole to offer honey in November 2009 when they knew that the nearby Croft Tearoom was opening. They had started keeping bees at their home in St Paul's Cray in October 2008. Grace had retired from teaching at a local school and David was winding down his career in chartered surveying. Their contact with Carole was mutually perfect timing because their successful production technique had yielded 100 lbs of honey that summer. That had left them with a lot of surplus – while Carole was keenly looking for local suppliers of quality food.

On her first visit Carole was very impressed with the neatly organised, clean and spotless home production process – and of course there was nil carbon footprint with Main Road situated so close to her Tearoom.

Grace and David stopped their production last year but they can readily pass on their extensive experience and knowledge of bee-keeping as indeed their friend and veteran bee-keeper Eric did for them as mentor when they first started. Membership of the Orpington Bee Association was another vital source of information, help and social friendship. As great lovers of their garden, of birds and wildlife, Grace and David gained huge enjoyment from their bee-keeping hobby. "But you've got to be committed. You need lots of patience and it is essential in summer to keep the discipline and routine." Customers at the Croft Tearoom have certainly testified that Cray Village Honey is tasty and delicious!

(4) Artisan Bread

In Carole's search for genuinely local suppliers to the Croft, one item constantly eluded her: hand-baked artisan bread (made only from flour, yeast, salt & water and without the use of processing aids or artificial additives found in commercial bakeries and supermarkets). A couple of suppliers were visited in Greenwich and Dulwich but she could not source anything made in the borough of Bromley!

However, in 2014 the Croft won a small grant from Sustain and Carole set up a 'Passion for Bread' project recruiting Dorota Das, a local mum and home-baker to set up and market the project. Another interested mum of two, Maria Taylor, got involved as a volunteer and Carole sent her on a training course in London to supplement her knowledge of sourdough bread baking.

Originally a teacher, Maria *(photo overleaf)* baked lovely breads in her home kitchen and she started supplying them to the Tearoom on Saturdays. Maria offered regular tastings and popular choices included sourdoughs, rye and spelt as well as a number of flavoured sourdoughs. Subsequently she set up her own microbakery 'The Bread and Butter Bakery' in Chislehurst. Maria has been involved in a number of community events teaching about sourdough and giving away sourdough starter so people can bake their own bread. Maria is passionate about healthy eating and so too are many of her regular customers at the Croft who enjoy her delicious hand-baked breads, including Carole and Norman!

Popular Events, Talks and Performers

From the Tearoom's photographic archives let us now revisit some of the past, very enjoyable events held at the Croft.

Morris Dancing

Arabian Nights, starring Naama Gelber, bellydancer.

Jazz with the Dave Silk Trio

Phil Waller – Tea & Talk, Orpington History

Sylvia Seaton playing at the Burns Night

Sylvia writes:

"I literally stumbled across the Croft by accident! I didn't know St Mary Cray High Street and after parking my car in Derry Downs, I saw this lovely Tearoom! A cup of tea and a rest was what I needed! I met Carole who was so friendly and welcoming. I decided that I would make a return visit and in fact I went many times. When Carole learned that I am a musician, you can guess what happened! – I found myself being recruited, very happily, to bring my violin and play at numerous Croft Tearoom events especially the annual Burns Night and Valentine's Day festivities.

I think that the Croft Tearoom is a wholly commendable set-up. It is such an asset to the local area. It looks neat and attractive and in keeping with the buildings nearby. The community aspect is so brilliant and important. I can pop in and always find lovely little gifts to buy. It is so much nicer and more satisfactory to think that I'm buying things that local people have made, instead of my money being swallowed up by one of the big faceless corporate stores. We are all one local community and it's so good that we have community hubs like the Croft where we can all meet and engage with each other".

Sylvia is leader of the Orpington Symphony Orchestra and with three of her local friends Becky, David and Philippa she is a member of the Ilyrica String Quartet.

Burns Night at the Tearoom: Barry the Piper (left) and David House in high spirits!

Artwork and Books

Local artists, craft workers, writers and publishers are most grateful that the Croft Tearoom has kindly stocked and sold their work.

Below and on the next pages we feature some of the local artwork and books that the Tearoom has kindly supported.

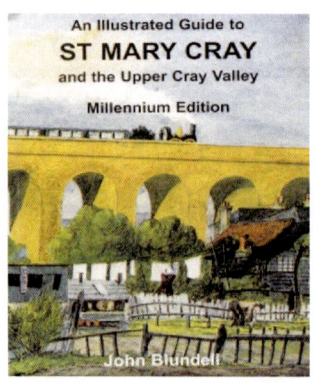

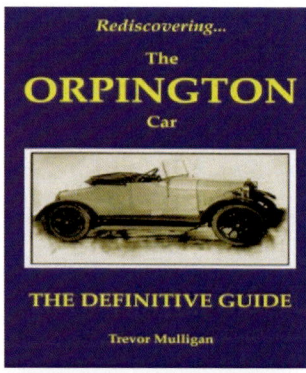

When we asked for a publicity photograph for the new book *Forever Amber* (history of Cray Wanderers Football Club) we never guessed that Carole's young volunteer at the Tearoom had the name Amber! *(See the name tag in the photograph: an amazing coincidence!)*

Dove on the Wing *book launch*

Cray Compendium *book launch*

Jocelyn Leigh

Jean Edwards

Poems

Three customers have been inspired to celebrate the Tearoom in verse ...

The Croft Tearoom

Raised from the rubble of a bygone era,
When community meant people chatting face to face
Over a cup of tea and maybe some cake:
Now you can't do that in cyber space.

T'is why the Croft Tearoom was built for this time,
A place to meet and rest, away from the herd,
You simply walk in, order, then take a seat:
All done without a forgotten password.

Richard Bowdery

Richard Bowdery lives in St Mary Cray. He has a lifelong keen interest in writing. His current activities include the roles of author, playwright, poet, community correspondent and on-line columnist / football blogger. Richard has given poetry presentations at the Croft.

The Croft Tearoom

The Croft has a ring to its name:
Where poets come to strut their stuff
And maybe find a path to fame.

But there's more to the Croft;
I'll have you know there's cake and tea,
Convivial chat and *bonhomie*!

This place where future poets come
To read and entertain,
To try their luck and have their say:
With our support and applause,
They go and follow their cause.

And as I leave to go,
I shake hands with those I know:
To fellow Croftians I bid *adieu, bon chance*
But I will be back
For the tea, cake and *craic*!

Les Cheeseman

Christmas 2014

For the Croft Poetry Club

Come now, heed my awful warning,
The poetry group meets on Thursday morning.
Assembling around about half past ten
They all eat cake and go home again.

Why do they come? I really don't care.
I know the reason that I am there.
I'm not there for learning's sake:
I'm just there to eat the cake!

I don't object to hearing rhymes.
I've had some very jolly times,
And I'm quite happy if I can
Munch away on marzipan!

The folk that go are all quite fun
Especially when they're eating bun.
But I wouldn't mind if they're not all nice
If I can partake of almond slice!

These folk aren't taken by the muse.
I think the poems are just a ruse
And though they all play their part
They're just after bakewell tart!

But here's the reason why I grizzle:
The Croft's run out of lemon drizzle!
And I am left feeling quite bereft
For finding that there's no cake left!

So, happy people, listen here,
I wish you all much good cheer
And, good Croft cooks please stay awake:
Now where's the blooming Christmas cake!

Steve Cotterell

Croft Poetry Club at Christmas.

The Croft Poetry Club

The Croft Poetry Club was founded in March 2014. It originated from the book launch *Dove on the Wing* (biography of Donald Ward, poet and pacifist) at the Croft in November 2013. When a large crowd filled the Tearoom for the launch, Carole inevitably started thinking: "Maybe there is potential for a Poetry Club in St Mary Cray?" The club has thrived! – it has more than twenty members on its books now. And the Croft Book Club, founded in 2015, is thriving too.

Steve Cotterell lives in Orpington and has given the Croft his volunteer help with social media. A lifelong enthusiast of butterflies and moths, Steve gave a Tea and Talk entitled Butterflies of St Mary Cray and Beyond. The audience heard about a species of butterfly that can cross the Atlantic. There is no limit to what you can learn at the Croft Tearoom!

Les Cheeseman has visited the Croft with his wife Val, travelling from their home in Mottingham. Les's artwork has been exhibited in Mottingham Library, and he has written a poem that was recited at the official unveiling of the new village sign. Les has recently passed his 80th birthday. He has always been a keen cyclist. He knows the value of comfortable Tearooms on the borders of London and Kent where hungry and thirsty cyclists can re-fuel!

Retirement and Relaunch Party – 29th May 2015

Here is a selection of photographs from the early evening party where customers and guests of the Croft Tearoom heard speeches from Carole Wells and Rebecca Birs to mark Carole's retirement from the Tearoom and Rebecca's arrival as the new owner and manager. The transfer of ownership was to take place at the end of June 2015.

A packed Tearoom heard speeches too from Jim Cook, Colin Maclean and Jerry Dowlen in tribute to Carole and the tremendous popularity and community spirit of her Tearoom. Gifts were presented to Carole and Rebecca to mark the respective retirement and relaunch.

Press Coverage of the Croft Tearoom

I am most grateful to the local press for kindly carrying news of the Tearoom which gave us valuable publicity.

**Catering for the Community:
Serving up regeneration in St Mary Cray**
Richard Bowdery for **Bromley Life** *magazine, Nov 2011.*

To rejuvenate an ailing urban area takes inspiration. For Carole Wells that inspiration was her mum.

Originally from Edinburgh, Carole started her working life as a careers advisor at a London borough council. Then in 1983, along with two colleagues, they set up a youth recruitment and training business. But a health scare in 2005 caused Carole to revaluate so she began to cast around for new opportunities, which is where her mum comes in. "One of the things that mum really enjoys is traditional afternoon tea," said Carole. But there was nowhere for me to take her when she visited. All I could find were cafés with plastic seats and no tablecloths."

Such places were not her mother's 'cup of tea'. And so came Carole's eureka moment – why not set up a traditional Tearoom that provided a friendly welcome, home-baking and good customer service in friendly surroundings. That was all the encouragement that Carole needed. She would set up the business as a social enterprise. Perhaps this latest initiative will help bring back the community spirit that everyone in St Mary Cray would like to see return.

Demolition, 2008

Environmental Tearoom Pouring Cash into Area
News Shopper, *18 Nov 2009*

An environmentally friendly Tearoom has just opened.

The Croft Tearoom in St Mary Cray High Street is surrounded by 17th century buildings and is in a conservation area. It has been built using sustainable timber, reclaimed roof tiles and recycled bricks. It has a heat recovery system. This works by trapping hot air inside the building and extracting cold, stale air. It then brings in fresh, cool air that mixes with the hot air inside.

Carole Wells who owns and manages the Tearoom said: "We are committed to the environment, trying to avoid food miles and supporting small producers and farmers. The Tearoom will provide a really lovely atmosphere with good quality food which is home-made."

Items on sale inside the Tearoom, such as honey, cheese and chutney all come from the local area. Mrs Wells said: "It is about engaging the community and giving people a nice place to come and visit."

Tea and History
Enterprising couple run archive centre with highly prized refreshments
Bromley Times, *11 Feb 2010*

A Tearoom that serves up local history with its snacks has been praised by Jo Johnson the Conservative parliamentary candidate for Orpington. [*Jo was elected as Orpington's MP in May 2010*].

Founded by Carole Wells and her husband Norman in November last year, the centre has been praised by Mr Johnson for its bid to attract more businesses to the area. Mr Johnson said that more businesses are needed in the deprived zone of St Mary Cray, which comprises the two wards Cray Valley East and West.

▲ **Since it opened in November, the Croft Tearoom has shown how entrepreneurs can regenerate the Cray Valley.**

Following his visit to the Tearoom, Jo said, "Carole Wells and her husband Norman have created a much-needed focal point for residents that benefits the whole community. There are great opportunities for businesses here in the Crays that entrepreneurs would be mad not to snap up."

Tearoom Wins Top Industry Certificate
Croft Tearoom in St Mary Cray is presented prestigious award by the Mayor
Tim Dickens in the **Bromley Times,** *25 May 2010*

The Croft Tearoom, in High Street St Mary Cray, was presented with the Joe Ellis Tearoom Guide Highly Recommended award by the Mayor of Bromley, Douglas Auld, last Thursday.

The author of the guide joined regular customers of the café at the event. Joe Ellis said: "The Croft Tearoom really deserves the guide's highest accolade. It uses local produce to provide excellent fare. I do not award the Highest Recommended certificate regularly, so it truly reflects how impressive this Tearoom is."

The award came in the same week that the Croft team received a rare five-star 'Scores on the Doors' hygiene rating from environmental health officials.

Croft Tearoom display at St Mary's Church Flower Festival

Champions of the Environment
News Shopper, *14 July 2010*

A Tearoom which judges said had made an 'enormous impact' in its community came out on top in Bromley's 21st Environmental Awards.

The Croft Tearoom in St Mary Cray scooped the overall winner gong at the awards evening held at the civic centre. It also won the Business Award for 'Sustainability'.

The prizes, handed out in 9 categories, recognise and reward local people who take pride in their environment and make a difference to the quality of life in the borough.

The Croft Tearoom beat more than 20 finalists to the overall award and was presented with its trophy by Roger Harrabin, the BBC's environmental analyst.

Business in Focus
Not just a Tearoom, Carole's cafe is base for whole community
Ben Caine **Bromley Times***, 25 Oct 2012*

An independent shop in St Mary Cray is making a big stir in the community.

Since 2009, the area has been home to the Croft Tearoom, managed by Carole Wells. With the UK economy suffering, Carole and her husband Norman took early retirement from their recruitment business to set up their new Tearoom.

Explaining why she chose St Mary Cray instead of other locations, Carole said: "We wanted to try and put something back into an area that needed it."

The Croft, which is a social enterprise, aims to offer an alternative to the large companies and chains populating most high streets.

Crucially, the business relies on a team of volunteers who rally around to make sure the owners and the staff can make the business come together, and Carole is always looking for more to grow the enterprise.

Letters to the Local Press

Local customers have used the Letters page of the *Kentish Times* newspaper to pay tribute to the Croft Tearoom.

Raise a cup and saucer to our past
Letter from Glenda Hay of St Mary Cray, Feb 2010

It is rare to see such an inspiring project as the Croft Tearoom.

In a day when traditional high streets and shopping parades seem to be overwhelmed by big businesses and out-of-town mega-complexes this is an important success. This not-for-profit enterprise has received praise from the political spectrum and seems to be a hit with residents. And it is a pleasure to read that the décor is not modern, tacky nor futuristic, but harks back to the good old days with a photograph of a young Margaret Thatcher *(visiting the 'Tip Top' bakery)* included in the local history display.

I am delighted to read that there are still people in our community that yearn for a bit of historical pride. The history of St Mary Cray and the surrounding areas is an open book and something we rarely turn the pages of. Generations of my family have grown up around here and I feel quite passionate about the area.

Tearoom that cheers
Letter from John Gamet of Keston, March 2010

Having recently visited the Croft Tearoom, I found it a joy to once again experience the atmosphere of an English tea shop. Bright, yet cosy, with friendly attentive staff, we were happy to enjoy an excellent cuppa from beautiful white china cups. I wish this non-profit-making project every success. St Mary Cray is fortunate to have a first-class tea shop.

Home cooking and community spirit
Letter from Jemima Pickford of Hayes, March 2010

I would like to write in support of businesses like the Croft Tearoom that were featured in the Bromley Times. As a community interest company the café stands up as exactly what we need in today's broken society. It creates jobs in the local community and provides a central point for people to come and socialise.

It seems that with a bit of community spirit, and some quality home cooking, we can start to make a difference.

Credo
Jehan Haddad

The Croft Tearoom has been a great help and a key supporter of Credo since May 2010 by offering to display and sell Credo's individual ceramic pieces at the café for an agreed amount of sale percentage. The Tearoom not only offers the prospect for Credo to sell the ceramics but also it gave the opportunity to one

Credo service user to volunteer and actively manage the process by individually choosing and pricing the items and liaising directly with the Tearoom's manager.

That role and the sales of the individuals' works help build their confidence and self-esteem which in turn has a great impact on their wellbeing.

Credo

Jehan Haddad is the Creative Arts and Learning Coordinator of Credo, a Community Options creative arts project, working with people who have experienced mental ill health.

Special Memories

Heather Kroiter
E-mail, June 2015

I was so excited that a Tearoom would be opening in St Mary Cray that I made sure I'd be there on the opening day. I wasn't a frequent visitor at that stage, but it became one of my favourites. As I kept visiting, I came to know the staff and knew that I could go there for lovely coffee and cake, and for company. It became a place I'd arrange to take or meet my friends. It was also pleasant because there was no intrusive music, just the happy hum of people chatting. Over the last year or two, I've been making sure that I visit at least once weekly to continue enjoying the friends and the food! Long may it continue :-)

Liz Johnston
Speaking at the Retirement & Relaunch Party, May 2015

I recall one person describing the Tearoom as "A little corner of heaven." And another good description was: "The Tearoom is just like the Tardis!" That is very apt when you stop and think about it. The Croft might look small from the outside – and from the inside – but there is always so much going on that it seems somehow to expand in size, just like the telephone box in the *Doctor Who* television series!

My role in a helping capacity to Carole at the Tearoom was Window Dresser – and I also took on the role of designing and printing the posters for the events.

Trevor Mulligan
E-mail, June 2015

In June 2013, I had the good fortune to be invited to give a talk at the Croft Tearoom, concerning my book about, and the story behind, the Orpington car. When Carole suggested the idea, I wasn't too sure about what I was letting myself in for but, with Carole's encouragement, I bit the bullet and said I'd have a go.

To my pleasant surprise and amazement, I got through the talk mostly unscathed. Being aware that I was a total novice at public speaking, Carole suggested that I link up with Phil Waller of the Orpington History Organisation, to present a two-pronged history afternoon at the Croft.

Carole was happy to let the two of us format our programme without any input from herself, and we came up with the approach that I would do a two-part talk about the history of the local car from the 1920s either side of a talk by Phil on the history of the town of Orpington prior to the introduction of the Frank Smith-designed car.

Had it not been for Carole's friendly gesture and invitation to give that talk, I may never have experienced the adrenalin rush of talking in front of a gathered audience. Despite my nerves I enjoyed that afternoon and it's all thanks to Carole.

Charmaine Bourton
E-mail, June 2015

My story is only really that I went to the opening day and when the press came to take a photo Carole said to me: "Come on Charmaine be in the photo!" I said that I wasn't anything to do with it, just wanted to be a supporter and Carole insisted I was in the photo – which appeared in the *News Shopper*!

It was so nice to be included like that!

Charmaine is standing second from left in the group photograph outside the Tearoom on the opening day in November 2009.

Tearoom Timeline

Carole's research has led her to conclude that it was between 1891 and 1894 that a building first originated at the address of 263 High Street, St Mary Cray where the Croft Tearoom now stands. Here is a fascinating list of information about previous occupants of the building and details of the neighbouring premises.

(Photo: 2007) The original building dates back to circa 1891 / 1894 when it was built as a Seed Shop selling produce from the neighbouring Rosecroft and Cockmannings Nurseries. The building was right on the High Street so pedestrians could easily purchase seeds, vegetables, fruits, flowers, plants and other horticultural items. St Mary Cray was a busy trading centre during the 19th century with shops and businesses of all descriptions and a larger population than Orpington!

The junction of the High Street and Kent Road used to be known locally as Reynolds Cross and a coach once left from here daily for Greenwich and London. Many of the buildings around the Tearoom include some fine 18th & 19th century houses (the Wealden House used to incorporate the 'Golden Teapot' stores!) and Pubs – including our neighbour The Red Lion which dates from 1756.

St Mary Cray nestles in the Cray Valley which follows the Cray River rising in Orpington and running into the Thames near Dartford. Many Roman and Anglo-Saxon remains have been found around the village and several parts, including the Tearoom are designated Conservation areas.

1891 Census

Population of St Mary Cray: 1,988 people.
Red Lion Inn listed.
265 High Street listed:
William (Billie) Buster – age 48 – Head of Household – Occupation: Nurseryman / Seedsman.
Lucy Lane – age 72 – Aunt – single, lived off own means.
Jane Dunn – age 71 – Servant / Nurse.
263 High Street not listed as existing.

1901 Census

Population of St Mary Cray: 1,894 people.
Red Lion Inn listed.
265 High Street listed as Rosecroft Cottage:
Lucy Lane – age 82 – Head - lived off own means.
Elizabeth Hamlin – age 68 – Servant / Domestic Nurse.
263 High Street listed as Seed Shop – uninhabited.

Note: In the *Bromley Directory* of 1901, George & James Lane are listed as Nurserymen in High Street (no number). Could be related to Lucy Lane?

Maps

1860s – 263 High Street not shown; 1894 – now it is shown (Old Maps website); 1896 – also shown. The map shows 'Nurseries' stretching back some way from Rosecroft Cottage and around what is now the Rosecroft Social Club.

Conclusion

263 High Street built between 1891 and 1894.

'Cray' pattern designed by William Morris(1834-1896). He lived in the 'Red House' in Bexleyheath between 1859-1865.

Date – Owner – Business

2007 to June 2015 - Circa Ltd (Carole and Norman Wells) – Tearoom and Shop

1987 to 2007 – Michael and Christine Wise – Crays Florists Shop

1980 to 1987 – Barton Keith Tarry – Crays Nursery (Eva Florence Gertrude Tarry)

1960 to 1980 – Edith Mary Beaumont – Crays Nursery (Florist & Farm Shop) (A. Beaumont – Bexleyheath)

c1937 to 1959 – Christian William Chantler – Rosecroft (possibly Cockmannings) Nursery

c1911 to 1936 – Arthur Hook (possibly Tenant) – Motor Engineer & Cycle Agents

1914 sold to Christian William Chantler

c1905 to 1914 – William (Billy) Lane Buster – Rosecroft Nursery.

c1894 to 1905 – (possibly) - Seed Shop

The three photographs on this and the preceding page show these former scenes:

One: A funeral, circa 1910 with the Rosecroft Nursery occupying the present-day site of the Croft Tearoom.

Two: Looking along the High Street circa 1900 with the Red Lion in the foreground, to the right.

Three: G. Feast the butcher's shop (with abattoir at the rear) in 1976, occupying the site across the road from the present-day Croft Tearoom.

Last Pour from the Teapot …

I still love visiting Tearooms and I enjoyed setting up and running my own. It was the best job ever and serving customers was truly a pleasure and a privilege.

I hope you have enjoyed reading my story and that you too will continue visiting the Croft as it evolves in the years to come. Let me finish with a quote that sums up for me the pleasure of 'taking tea':

"The very ritual of tea-making, warming the pot, making sure that the water is just boiling, inhaling the fragrant steam, arranging the tea-cosy to fit snugly around the precious container, all the preliminaries lead up to the exquisite pleasure of sipping the brew from thin porcelain, and helping oneself to hot buttered scones and strawberry jam, a slice of feather-light sponge cake or home-made shortbread."
Miss Read, *Gossip from Thrush Green.*

Cray 150 Publications

Cray 150 Publications aims to publish local interest books and to organise or support local events relating to the arts and heritage of Orpington and the Crays.

This book *The Croft Tearoom 2007-2015* is our latest product.

You can find out more about us from our website or by enquiry at the Croft Tearoom.

www.cray150publications.co.uk